# The Yorkshire Dales
## and the Peak District

Books by W.A. Poucher
available from Constable

*Scotland*
*Wales*
*The Lake District*
*The Highlands of Scotland*
*The Alps*
*The magic of Skye*
*The Scottish Peaks*
*The Peak and Pennines*
*The Lakeland Peaks*
*The Welsh Peaks*

Other books now out of print

*The backbone of England*
*Climbing with a camera*
*Escape to the hills*
*A camera in the Cairngorms*
*Scotland through the lens*
*Highland holiday*
*The North Western Highlands*
*Lakeland scrapbook*
*Lakeland through the lens*
*Lakeland holiday*
*Lakeland journey*
*Over lakeland fells*
*Wanderings in Wales*
*Snowdonia through the lens*
*Snowdon holiday*
*Peak panorama*
*The Surrey hills*
*The magic of the Dolomites*
*West country journey*
*Journey into Ireland*

# Malham Cove

*(frontispiece)*

The most magnificent rock scenery in the Pennines, these overhanging crags are more than 300 feet high. The river now emerges from their base, but in past ages it plunged over the lip of the crags as an immense waterfall.

# THE YORKSHIRE DALES
# & THE PEAK DISTRICT

## W.A.Poucher

Constable London

First published in Great Britain 1984
by Constable and Company Limited
10 Orange Street London WC2H 7EG
Copyright © 1984 by W.A. Poucher
ISBN 0 09 465550 2
Reprinted 1984
Text filmset by Servis Filmsetting Ltd
Printed and bound in Great Britain by
W.S. Cowell Ltd Ipswich

# The photographs

# Preface

During the last half-century I have climbed the Pennine Peaks, tramped lonely moors and ambled through many lovely dales in an attempt to capture their beauty with my cameras. The Yorkshire Dales, in particular, fascinated me with their astonishing variety: precipitous limestone outcrops such as Malham Cove; rivers whose cascades glitter in the sunlight, like the Aysgarth Falls; and tranquil villages whose smooth greens are the prettiest in the country. The Peak District is quite different and more austere – a national park famous for its narrow defiles, such as Dovedale, and its vertical Edges, some of which, like Stanage, stretch for four miles. Though the whole region is a great draw for the tough walker, the Edges, dominated by the flattish top of Kinder Scout, are a special magnet for the rock climber.

Those who live in the great cities, such as Sheffield, which surround these beautiful places are fortunate to be able to reach them so easily, to walk through such scenic glories, breathe the pure air, and observe with delight the changing colours of the landscape from spring to winter.

The photographs in this book, which were all taken with Leica cameras, are arranged from south to north – from Dovedale to Hadrian's Wall – and I have chosen particularly those which appeal to me as characterizing the unique splendours of the region. Should any reader desire more details about climbing the crags portrayed here, these will be found in my guide-book, *The Peak & Pennines*.

W.A. Poucher
4 Heathfield
Reigate Heath
Surrey
1984

# Dovedale

One of the loveliest dales in the Peak District
National Park, it is threaded by a rippling stream
famous with anglers, and the tors and limestone
pinnacles that adorn the valley walls have
become a major attraction for rock climbers in
the past decade. In this photograph, the little
peak of Thorpe Cloud is seen dominating the
beginning of the narrow dale, which extends
proper for three miles and ends at Dove Holes.
From there the river passes through Hartington
and rises on Axe Ridge near Buxton, nearly 15
miles away.

# Thor's cave

This cave displays some remarkable features: the arch is symmetrical, 30 feet high and 23 feet wide, and the roof is supported by massive limestone columns deep in the interior. To facilitate entrance, since the cave opening is 250 feet above the road, steps have been built; and the cave, which is the most attractive feature of the Manifold Valley (running almost parallel with Dovedale), may be reached from Ilam or from Wetton.

# The Railway Slab

This slab is passed on the left during the approach to the Black Rocks of Cromford: my picture captures a gymnastic ascent by an unroped climber.

# The Black Rocks of Cromford

*(overleaf)*

These prominent gritstone crags lie to the south of Matlock Bath. Their spectacular summit platform, which on a clear day gives a panoramic view of the whole Matlock district, can be reached easily by the ordinary pedestrian.

# *Cratcliff Tor*

Walkers heading north from Winster towards Bakewell will see this gritstone outcrop on the far horizon. Closer inspection will reveal the Hermit's Cave, which is railed in and contains a crucifix: its position is marked by two yews on the south-west corner of the cliffs. There are many courses for the rock climber, of which the most famous is the Owl Gully, a V-shaped rift splitting the prominent buttress on the extreme right of the picture.

# Robin Hood's Stride

Two fluted pinnacles, some 30 feet apart, can
just be seen rising from the trees which
surround this gritstone outcrop standing in
open ground to the west of Cratcliff Tor. Robin
Hood must have been a giant to have stepped
across the gap between those pinnacles!

# Birchen's Edge

*(overleaf)*

The eastern Edges of the Peak District extend north for some fifteen miles along the lofty rim of the Derwent Valley from Chatsworth to Ladybower Reservoir, forming the precipitous lip to vast stretches of moorland to the east. To their west, the ground falls steeply away to the streams that thread the valley floor. Birchen's Edge (seen here, with beginners training) lies near the southern end of the chain and is crowned by Nelson's slender monument. It is easily reached from the nearby Robin Hood Inn on the A619.

# Froggatt Edge

*(overleaf p 26)*

Named after the hamlet immediately below it, this is scenically superior to many other Edges and is characterized by the Pinnacle, a square gritstone tower separated from it by a deep gully, seen in this picture. Froggatt Edge may be reached from the Chequers Inn on the B6054.

# Three Pebble Slab

*(overleaf p 27)*

This is an ascent where delicate movements are vital. A climber is just setting off, roped to the leader at the top of the slab.

# Lawrencefield

Immediately to the south of the Surprise View
(see next picture) this small quarry lies hidden.
In this frontal view of the Great Wall and Pool,
Excalibur is the vertical crack on the right of
the Wall. There are other climbing courses on
Gingerbread Slab, extreme right.

# The Surprise View

*(overleaf)*

As the A625, one of the many roads intersecting the Edges, descends to Hathersage by way of Millstone Edge Nick, the famous view is suddenly disclosed – its name doubtless arises from the unexpected change of scene from desolate moorland to the glorious panorama of the High Peak.

# Millstone Edge

As one drives up from Hathersage to the Surprise View, this great rock barrier crowns the horizon on one's left. It was once an immense quarry, and is most spectacularly seen on a sunny afternoon when shadows cast by the sharp corners of the vertical gritstone walls outline its succession of bays. This picture shows the bay to the left of the Embankment in the Great North Road area.

# Carl Wark

*(overleaf)*

This is an ancient fortress whose primitive
fortifications can still be seen, merging with the
moorland and bracken. It is a prominent
outcrop of gritstone in the valley threaded by
Burbage Brook, hemmed in on the east by the
long line of Burbage Rocks, on the north-west
by the loftier Higger Tor, and to the south-west
by the sloping moor that terminates abruptly at
Millstone Edge. Sloping up from west to east,
the crest ends in a conspicuous prow. Carl
Wark can be reached by many tracks through
the bracken, and most directly from the bridge
over Burbage Brook.

# Burbage Edge

*(overleaf p 36)*

This Edge faces Carl Wark (previous picture)
and is much broken up by boulders. The
climbers are on Ash Tree Wall.

# Saturday at Stanage Edge

*(overleaf p 37)*

This magnificent escarpment of gritstone runs
north from the Cowper Stone for about four
miles, forming the western lip of Hallam Moor.
Many tracks lead towards it through the heather
from the narrow Hathersage-to-Bamford road,
and approaching the Edge this way the walker
sees a long wall of serrated cliffs on the skyline.
These vary in height between 20 and 80 feet,
the lower ones being at the northern end of the
escarpment between High Neb and Stanage
End.

# Two famous climbs

Inverted V is on the left, and the Right Hand Buttress on the right. Ropes show the line taken by the climbers.

# Caves on Robin Hood's Balcony

*(overleaf)*

Any agile walker can safely descend from the ridge to inspect these remarkable caves.

# High Neb

These prominent crags are reached by turning
left at the exit of Jacob's Ladder (a rock
staircase in the gap that carries the old Roman
Road down into the valley) and strolling along
a safe, high path. Many discarded millstones can
be found in the bracken below these cliffs.

# A reservoir seen from Derwent Edge

This last and most northerly of the eastern barriers of the Peak District frowns upon the blue waters of Ladybower and Derwent Reservoirs. It differs from the Edges already described in that it offers no continuous façade of gritstone but has strange outcrops of rock which stand in splendid isolation on the very edge of the moor. Their existence here, in this otherwise bare stretch of country, poses an intriguing geological problem. This photograph was taken from Whitstone Lee Tor on the rim of Derwent Edge, a viewpoint that may be reached by paths from Ashopton or Cutthroat Bridge on the A57.

# The Wheel Stones

*(overleaf)*

Leaving the last viewpoint, the walker will see these remarkable rocks on the far skyline. They are worth close inspection, and a well-trodden path leads to them across the moor.

# The Salt Cellar

The path continues due north, and after passing
White Tor on the left, the walker should keep a
sharp lookout for this extraordinary rock
formation, just off the ridge on the left. Unless
you are a good rock climber, do not attempt to
climb to the top as you may have some
difficulty in getting down again!

# Back Tor

This tor marks the end of the walk which has
encompassed the previous two unusual rock
formations. To the north lies typical Peak
moorland, and to the west the walker will have
a good view of the summit ridge of Bleaklow.

# Limestone cliffs of Stoney Middleton

*(overleaf)*

The most spectacular section of the A623 runs through Middleton Dale, where the twisting road descends gradually through a narrow ravine, hemmed in to the south by limestone quarries whose white dust powders the vivid green of dense vegetation, and to the north by this long line of stupendous vertical limestone cliffs. These end abruptly at the little village of Stoney Middleton. Though the tall cliffs overhang the road, the passing motorist often misses them because of the thick belt of trees and steep grassy bank beside the highway. This picture was taken from the high ground at the south side of the ravine.

# Windhover and Aurora

These are two of the climbs that start from the base of the towering limestone cliffs: this picture is a telephoto shot taken from the same viewpoint as the previous picture.

# Conksbury Bridge

*(overleaf)*

The Lathkill is one of the loveliest rivers in the Peak District, with a wealth of little weirs whose waterplay adds to the charm of a walk through the dale. Like many streams in the limestone district, it disappears in places and runs underground. Though it rises in a hole in the side of Ricklow Dale, there is very little water in its bed till it reaches Over Haddon. By the time it reaches this beautiful bridge (to the south of Bakewell and west of Rowsley) the river is wider; and it continues to Alport where the dale ends.

# Lathkill Dale

The most enchanting section of this dale is
easily reached from Conksbury Bridge (previous
picture), for a path runs beside the quietly
flowing stream which is a paradise for the
angler. At the top of the hill on the right of the
picture, the cottages of Over Haddon can just
be seen.

# Ashford Bridge
*(overleaf)*

The River Wye flows through a succession of narrow limestone dales with some of the most beautiful scenery in the Peak District. It rises in the dim recesses of Pool's Cavern in Buxton and, after passing the bridge seen here, it meanders through tree-studded meadows near Ashford, Bakewell and Haddon, finally joining the Derwent at Rowsley.

# Monsal Dale

Monsal Head, standing high above the dale, affords the best viewpoint for admiring it. The great railway viaduct seen in this picture once carried trains to Buxton but after the line was closed it was taken over by the Peak Planning Board, and it now carries the Monsal Trail, from which the walker can overlook the dale.

The many tunnels along the Trail are closed, but most are circumvented by paths.

# Raven Tor

*(overleaf)*

Miller's Dale contains many limestone outcrops which are known to rock climbers as Water cum Jolley. This enormous overhanging wall, which rises beyond Litton Mill, is 170 feet high: passing the conspicuous Prow is the most difficult section of the climb.

# Chee Tor

*(overleaf p 65)*

This sheer limestone precipice, on the left of the path beyond Miller's Dale station, is a favourite with the rock climbing fraternity.

# The end of Chee Dale

*(overleaf pp 66/67)*

Beyond the Tor shown in the previous picture the path continues through a narrow section of the dale beside the river where the well-known Stepping Stones help keep the walker's feet dry. The pinnacles and buttresses seen in this photograph suddenly appear on the left, and mark the end of the spectacular Wye Dale.

# The Goyt Valley

This beautiful valley has always been a magnet for the walker, and some years ago the motor traffic problem was solved by making the road a one-way single-track route for cars. The upper section of the valley, reached after passing the last trees, is the most picturesque, with colourful moors rising to the horizon on both sides of the river. This picture shows the point where the stream enters the trees with the Goytsclough Quarry on the left. The quarry is the best place to leave a car: from there, walk alongside the river to Derbyshire Bridge on the old Macclesfield road, or take one of the many tracks rising up on to the moors, where the whole scene opens up to perfection.

# Goyt Bridge

*(overleaf)*

Many tracks lead over the surrounding moors from this famous and picturesque bridge.

# Hen Cloud

This shapely eminence rises to the north-west of the charming hamlet of Upper Hulme, lying to the west of the A53. It rises steeply from the moor and is crowned with a ring of symmetrical buttresses which combine with its pyramidal form to give it a semblance of a real mountain. Some crags afford exciting scrambling, and there are at least three courses to attract the rock climber.

# The Roaches

*(overleaf)*

This picture of the Roaches, a favourite haunt
of expert rock climbers, was taken from the
road below Hen Cloud. The Roaches are
divided into two distinct bands of rock. Into
the base of the lower tier has been built the
Gamekeeper's Cottage, embowered in trees; to
its left stone steps lead up to the more level
ground which flanks the upper tier. Of this the
titanic slab of the Sloth, with its gigantic
overhang, is the most fantastic feature.

# Joe Brown
# on the Sloth

Taken from an adjoining buttress, this photograph shows the famous rock climber swinging from the overhang, with John Amatt waiting below on the Pedestal.

# The Winnats

(overleaf)

A steep road threads the entire length of this ravine near Castleton, hemmed in on both sides by limestone pinnacles. At one time ideal for testing motor cars, it is now in general use because the main road below Mam Tor has become impassable.

# The Great Ridge from Mam Tor

This great barrier rising between Castleton and Edale, the only one of its kind in the Peak District, is also known as the Mam Tor–Lose Hill Ridge. It looks its best from the cliffs of Mam Tor, as seen here. Almost four miles long, with a dilapidated stone wall running along its crest, the ridge may be reached from many paths, starting from almost any point. Seen in the distance in this picture is Back Tor, most prominent feature of the ridge.

# Edale Church and Grindsbrook

*(overleaf)*

Edale is the starting point for the Pennine Way, the 250-mile-long mountain walk which ends on the Scottish Border. After leaving the village, the Way rises along the slopes of Grindsbrook, seen in the background of this photograph.

# A grough on Kinder Scout

The Kinder plateau is full of groughs like the
one in this picture, and crossing them in a
direct line, even with a compass, is a most
difficult procedure. When making for the
downfall, it is advisable to find the Kinder
River and follow it down.

# The Boxing-glove Stones

*(overleaf)*

These strange stones are encountered on the path round the edge of the Kinder plateau, possibly the most beautiful walk in this area

# Prominent stakes mark the Pennine Way

Leaving the crest of the Snake, the Pennine Way is obvious and marked with stakes, like those seen here. If the mist rolls down to blot out everything, crossing Bleaklow can be a hazardous experience; the going is safer on a clear day, but the only landmark that can be relied on is that of the Wain Stones (see following picture).

# The Wain Stones

*(overleaf)*

The Pennine Way passes these conspicuous stones a few hundred yards before reaching Bleaklow Head; from the stones there are excellent views, with the foreground sloping down to a string of reservoirs.

# The Cow and Calf on Ilkley Moor

The town of Ilkley is spread along the banks of the River Wharfe and frowned upon from the south by the brim of its famous moor. As a lofty stretch of wild country, this is popular with ramblers and opens up to the north extensive views of Wharfedale, backed by Blubberhouses Moor. But it is also a favourite venue of the rock climber, since it exhibits three groups of crags, two of which consist of eroded gritstone and the third of sandstone. All of them flank the rim of the moor and are situated about one mile from the centre of the town. The Cow is a well-defined buttress about 100 feet high and the Calf a gigantic boulder below it, as seen in this picture.

# Rock climbing on Josephine

*(overleaf)*

Often used for training purposes, this climb is on the north wall of the sandstone quarry on Ilkley Moor.

## Brimham Rocks

The Double Idol estimated to weigh two tons, is perfectly poised and balanced on a base only twelve inches in diameter.

# Crown Rock and Kissing Chair

The top of Brimham Moor abounds in huge gritstone rocks such as these. The moor, owned by the National Trust, covers an area of some 60 acres, is about three miles east of Pately Bridge and is easily reached from Wharfedale. Its collection of fantastic rocks should delight any photographer.

# The Turtle

*(overleaf)*

This extraordinary rock, easily found, is a good example of the formations to be seen on Brimham Moor.

# The Dancing Bear

his rock is near the Druid's Idol: besides
aking a good photograph, it is also a
vourite with climbers.

# Stump Cross Caverns

*(overleaf)*

The entrance to these caves is 1,100 feet above
sea-level, on the south side of the wild,
windswept moorland road (B6265) that connect
Grassington with Pateley Bridge. The cave
contain almost every type of calcite formation,
all very well illuminated: this example is known
as the Butcher's Shop.

# Bolton Abbey, Wharfedale

Wharfedale, an enchanting valley and possibly the most beautiful in Yorkshire, lies in the bosom of the Pennines. Its spacious curves, stretching northwards from the very threshold of great industrial cities, peter out in the distant fastnesses of the hills about Outershaw. The lower section (as far as Threshfield and Grassington) is richly wooded and dotted with historic buildings. The explorer should begin with Bolton Abbey, seen here: the transepts and choir are in ruins, but the grounds are still very beautiful. Bolton Hall stands just behind the Abbey, and the manor is held by the Dukes of Devonshire.

# The Strid
*(overleaf)*

Some two miles north of Bolton Abbey, the visitor may leave his car beside the road and descend through Bolton Woods to the swirling, chattering Strid. No attempt should be made to leap across the narrow channel through which the water rushes, since a fall might well result in loss of life.

# Barden Tower

This beautiful and massive ruin is no more than
a keep: at times it is part-occupied.

# Kilnsey Crag

This conspicuous crag, appearing ahead in the drive northwards, is famous for the great difficulty of its ascent – particularly of the large overhang.

# Close view
# of the overhang

*(overleaf)*

The extent of the crag is surprising: it is in fact the eastern terminus of The Craven Fault, and at its highest is 200 feet. The roof of the overhang juts out 35 feet from the vertical limestone wall.

# Kettlewell

The Bridge on the left of this picture has been painted and photographed innumerable times, affording as it does the best foreground for a view of this charming village, much loved by hikers for its quaint cottages and inns. The bridge stands astride a pretty, gurgling beck.

# Hubberholme Church

Leading north, the road keeps to the east bank
of the River Wharfe. On reaching Buckden, the
visitor will find it worthwhile turning left and
driving along a narrow road to see this church,
famous for its rood loft which is one of the few
surviving in England.

## Malham Cove

*(overleaf)*

This magnificent limestone outcrop is the
spectacular showpiece of the Pennines: the cliffs
are more than 300 feet high, and the rim (over
which in bygone days a waterfall plunged) now
overhangs by some 14 feet. The Cove is a
gigantic semi-circle of overhanging precipices,
striated vertically by the action of the water and
frost, with Malham Beck emerging as a
substantial stream at its foot. Through trees
covering the slope to either side, a path rises to
the summit platform of the Cove. Thousands of
visitors leave their vehicles in the car-park on
the edge of Malham village, and a gentle stroll
brings them to a splendid frontal view of this
geological masterpiece.

## The Cove
## from the rim

*(overleaf pp 120/121)*

This is the most comprehensive view of the
Cove from its rim. The original path kept close
to the cliffs, but a new one has now been made,
further away through the trees.

# Limestone pavement above the Cove

It needs a steady head if the visitor is to walk
along the edge of the precipice, but it is worth
the effort, for there soon appears ahead this
striking limestone pavement – the finest
example I know of.

# The approach to Gordale Scar

Leaving the village green in Malham, the road
forks: the left branch rises up to Malham Tarn,
but the right one (known as Mastiles Lane)
soon leads into the hills, with Gordale Scar on
the left.

# Gordale Scar

*(overleaf)*

The narrow entrance to this limestone defile cannot be seen until the walker approaches the S-shaped cliffs, whose towering walls are more than 200 feet high. The gorge can only be entered for a short distance before the walker is confronted by a waterfall. During dry weather there is very little water in this, and it is fairly easy to scramble up the rib on the right and gain access to the upper part of the chasm, but when the beck is in spate it is better not to try it. Rock climbers have been drawn to these cliffs since 1956, the last cliff to be conquered being the prodigious overhanging one on the right.

# Penyghent

*(overleaf pp 128/129)*

Seen from anywhere in upper Ribblesdale, this mountain has an attractive appearance with its smooth grassy slopes and small limestone outcrops. It rises gently for about two miles from Plover Hill in the north to its summit ringed with gritstone crags. Though the ridge may be easily attained from almost any point, it is usually climbed from Horton in Ribblesdale, and the most interesting ascent takes in two of the potholes with which the surrounding countryside is riddled.

# Hull Pot during a wet spell

The first pothole encountered on the ascent of Penyghent is Hull Pot, whose yawning mouth occupies a depression in the moor. Its roof collapsed centuries ago, leaving a hole 60 feet deep, 60 yards long, and 20 yards wide, now surrounded by a fence and derelict stone wall doubtless built to prevent sheep falling in.

During dry weather the beck above it disappears in a 'sink', but in a wet spell most of the water floods over the ground to cascade into the gash.

## Hunt Pot during a dry spell

This pothole lies about 200 yards to the south of Hull Pot, and on slightly higher ground. Though the surface depression is 60 yards wide, the gullet proper is only 15 feet long and six feet wide at the centre. A jammed boulder at the western end allows the wayfarer to stand over the chasm and look into its sinister depths; the sides are covered with moss, ferns and lichen in great profusion.

## Morning mist on Ingleborough

*(overleaf)*

This mountain is one of the great landmarks of the Pennines, and dominates the vast moorland triangle based upon Ingleton and Settle. The summit is a square, almost level, gritstone cap, but being part of the Craven Highlands it stands on an immense bed of limestone which is riddled with potholes – both the massif itself and the surrounding hills and dales. Four routes to its summit start from Clapham, Ingleton, Chapel-le-Dale and Selside; any two may be used for ascent and descent.

# One of the Norber Erratics

On the south-eastern flanks of Ingleborough is
a heterogeneous collection of Silurian boulders
which were deposited during the Ice Age – this
poised boulder is typical of them. They can
weigh up to 20 tons and many stand on
limestone pedestals. They may conveniently be
reached from Settle, Clapham, or by way of the
hamlet of Austwick.

# Gaping Gill Hole

*(overleaf)*

This is the finest pothole in Britain, its grim, precipitous, ferny walls plunging 340 feet (past the notorious ledge at 190 feet) to the Great Hall at the bottom. This main chamber is one of the largest in the world, with a floor space of half an acre. Into the pothole flows Fell Beck, whose tributaries rise on the slopes of Ingleborough and Simon Fell: once the stream reaches limestone it begins to sink in its bed, but the unabsorbed water runs into Gaping Gill, whose mouth, roughly circular in shape, could take a horse and cart without touching the sides. The pothole is not fenced in any way; a glance into its depths should be enough for most adventurers, though it can be closely inspected by those who do not suffer from vertigo.

# *Ingleborough from the sheepfold*

From Gaping Gill Hole, walkers making the
ascent of Ingleborough should cross the boggy
ground to reach its southern spur. At the
sheepfold seen in this picture the mountain's flat
summit is revealed for the first time.

# The flat summit of the peak
*(overleaf)*

Continuing the walk from Gaping Gill Hole, bear to the right and pick up the track that rises gently to the summit, in the centre of which is a well-built shelter. This is surmounted by an indicator, erected by the Ingleton Fell Rescue team to commemorate the coronation of Queen Elizabeth II on 2 June 1953.

# Alum Pot
## from Long Churn

The most interesting route down Ingleborough
goes by way of Simon Fell to the conspicuous
clump of trees, seen in the middle distance of
this photograph, surrounding Alum Pot – an
impressive, ugly chasm down which a stream
falls in a single plunge of 210 feet. Long Churn,
in the foreground, is a side-passage of Alum
Pot and can be used in its descent, needing only
half the 300 feet of rope-ladder necessary to
descend Alum Pot itself.

# The summit ridge of Whernside

Whernside is the highest mountain in this part of the Pennines, rising to the north-west of Ribblesdale Station on the B6255, its grassy summit ridge sloping gently from the south, a high stone wall running along its crest. It has no special features, but its ascent from the Hill Inn above Chapel-le-Dale makes a pleasant afternoon walk. Together with Penyghent and Ingleborough, this peak is the scene of the famous Three Peaks Race, covering 22 miles and with 4,500 feet of ascent and descent.

# West Burton

*(overleaf)*

Those who love the tranquil beauty of the Yorkshire Dales should drive over the hills from Buckden in Wharfedale to the enchanting village of West Burton in Wensleydale, at the entrance to the subsidiary Walden Dale. Here they can wander in peace round the cottages, shop and inn which are delightfully placed round the village green with its 1820 Monument and well-preserved stocks.

# Upper Aysgarth Fall

From West Burton the traveller should drive to
the first inn on the A684, the main highway
through Wensleydale. Here a right turn will
bring into view the rushing cascades on the
River Ure. The Upper Fall, shown here, can
best be seen from the first bridge.

# The Middle Fall

After driving on to the railway bridge, where
he may leave the car, the visitor can walk along
a nearby path through the trees to see the
Middle Fall.

# The beautiful Lower Fall

*(overleaf)*

When the River Ure is in spate (as seen in this photograph) the Lower Fall is without doubt one of the most splendid scenes of waterplay in the country. To view it to perfection, descend the bank and walk out to a dry rock: there you will not get wet and may enjoy to the full the magnificence and the music of the glittering cascades.

# Castle Bolton

The road leads by the way of Carperby to
Castle Bolton on the northern slopes of
Wensleydale: built in the fourteenth century, it
was the home and stronghold of the Scropes.

# Bainbridge
village green
*(overleaf)*

This is another enchanting village, with trees and cottages grouped round the green at intervals, and stocks on the grass in the centre.

# Hardrow Force

As a farewell to Wensleydale, nothing can
surpass a visit to Hardrow Force, lying in a
deep depression on the northern slopes of the
dale. On payment of a small fee, the visitor
passes through the parlour of the Green Dragon
Inn, walks along a narrow dale beside Fossdale
Gill, and after turning the last bend is
confronted with the fall itself. In one
uninterrupted drop of nearly 100 feet, it plunges
from the rim of limestone that overhangs the
receding banks of soft shale.

# Cautley Crag and Spout

*(overleaf)*

From Wensleydale, drive westwards to the
beautiful Rawthey Valley via Garsdale. From
the layby near the Cross Keys Hotel (seen here)
is a splendid prospect: the Calf, which
dominates the Howgills, towers on the western
skyline, with the imposing ring of Cautley Crag
below it, and Cautley Spout immediately to the
right. Those wishing to take a closer look may
cross the footbridge below the layby and follow
the path to the falls in their narrow cleft in the
green hillside.

# Butter Tubs

The pass familiarly known by this name links upper Wensleydale with Swaledale to the north. Having crossed wild expanses of moorland to reach the col between Great Shunner Fell and Lovely Seat, the road drops down into Swaledale past the 'Tubs'. These are infant potholes with peculiarly fluted sides and flat-topped pinnacles, all worn away by water trickling down the soft limestone.

# *Swaledale – Tan Hill Inn*

Swaledale is one of the least frequented dales in the Pennines, and its upper reaches are particularly wild and little-known. Though the road beyond Muker is narrow and tortuous with little to offer the motorist, the surrounding countryside is ideal tramping-ground for the tough walker. When thirsty, he can climb up to

Tan Hill Inn, reputed to be the highest pub in Britain.

# The Tees
# at Barnard Castle

*(overleaf)*

Teesdale is a more spacious valley than the
others previously described, and its finest
scenery begins at Barnard Castle, ending at
Cross Fell on the borders of Cumbria. The
town is beautifully situated on the northern
banks of the Tees, which is spanned by a
graceful medieval bridge: it is dominated by the
grand ruin of the castle, scene of Sir Walter
Scott's *Rokeby*, and once the home of the Balliol
family.

# High Force

North-west of Middleton-in-Teesdale is this
impressive waterfall, best seen when the river is
in spate, as in this picture. The falls can be
viewed from above by climbing the steps on the
right of the two great bastions of basalt.

# Caldron Snout

*(overleaf)*

This photograph was taken from the western side of the Snout, and shows the dam above the turbulent rapids. This remarkable scene can be reached by turning left just before the hotel at Langdon Beck, and following the road across the moor to Cow Green Reservoir. A path leads downhill to the large dam, below which there is a footbridge on the Pennine Way.

# Looking down the Caldron

This shot was taken from the same spot as the previous picture. Walkers who wish to see the bottom of the falls should follow the track opposite, on the eastern side of the Snout.

# Dufton Pike from the village green

*(overleaf)*

The high-level walk from Caldron Snout over the crest of the Pennines is for tough walkers only, who will discover that it unfolds not only views of striking grandeur and desolate moors, but one of the greatest surprises in the British hills (see following picture). This section of the Pennine Way ends at the charming and picturesque village of Dufton, whose green is dominated by the conical Dufton Pike, as seen in this photograph.

# High Cup Nick

This spectacular gash in the hillside is surrounded by basaltic columns and pinnacles, and on a clear day gives a view of the Lakeland peaks in the distant west. Though the Pennine Way passes this gigantic natural feature, it is most usually seen by walkers from Dufton who would not undertake the arduous walk from Caldron Snout. High Cup Nick is about four miles due east of Dufton; the walk up to it is an easy gradient all the way, and is marked by cairns where it crosses the open moor. It finishes at the watershed, where a cairn and indicator point the way to Caldron Snout.

# The terminal basaltic columns

This photograph, taken from the end of the Nick, looks west to the Vale of Eden, and to the Lakes beyond.

# Cross Fell from Milburn Grange

*(overleaf)*

Cross Fell is the highest hill in the Pennines, and stands just inside the Cumbria boundary. It does not make an imposing skyline, for there is little difference in height between it and its satellites: this view from Milburn Grange is the one where they are most clearly seen. The ground to the west of Cross Fell falls gently, backed by the distant Lakeland fells; in every other direction the Fell is flanked by vast stretches of boggy moorland best left alone by the walker.

# The mountain road to Great Dun Fell

This approach to Cross Fell terminates at a noticeboard some 300 feet below the radio station which surmounts Great Dun Fell. Beyond this the ground opens up, and Cross Fell can be seen on the far side of Little Dun Fell, in direct line with it. The walk to this point is easy but beyond this is the vast quagmire of Tees Head which requires careful negotiation before reaching a grassy break in the scree, leading to the summit of Cross Fell.

# The lonely summit of Cross Fell

On attaining the summit, it is still a long walk
northwards before the summit cairn is reached,
but in clear weather there is then a superb
panorama in all directions.

# The cliffs of
# Crag Lough

*(overleaf)*

Known formerly as High Shield Crags, this playground of the rock climber is less than half a mile long and forms a section of the northern escarpment of Hadrian's Wall. The eastern end of the Crags overlooks a blue, reedy tarn backed by Kielder Forest; the western end is only a short distance from Steel Rigg car-park, which may easily be reached from the famous Twice Brewed Inn on the B6318.

# Hadrian's Wall approach to Crag Lough

From Steel Rigg car-park the wayfarer can walk
along the Wall itself, or tramp along beside it,
passing Milecastle 39 en route.

# Climbers
# on the Pinnacle

*(overleaf)*

This detached needle of rock stands to the west of the Appian Way (a short break in the cliffs), and is easily climbed.

# The vertical crags
# above the Lough

*(overleaf p 193)*

The cliffs are splendidly placed to give a perfect view of the Lough.

# Hadrian's Wall

*(overleaf pp 194/195)*

This well-known barrier extends more than 73 miles from Wallsend-on-Tyne to Bowness-on-Solway, and makes an excellent long walk from end to end. But its most interesting section lies along the Pennine Way between Thirlwall and Housesteads, and about halfway between Crag Lough and Housesteads is Cuddy Crag, a superb viewpoint from which this photograph was taken.

# Housesteads

The carefully preserved ruins of this Roman camp are well worth a visit. As it is only two miles from Crag Lough, many walkers will approach it this way; drivers may park their cars at New Beggarbog on the north side of the B6318, and take a short walk across the fields to the ruins. This photograph shows the granary pillars which once supported the floor of the barn in which the legion's corn was stored.

# Calm after
# the storm
*(overleaf)*

A brilliant rainbow appears after the passing of
the notorious Helm Wind which blows up
sudden storms in the far north of England.